W9-AYR-676

TOP 10 BASKETBALL THREE-POINT SHOOTERS

John Albert Torres

SPORTS TOP 10

Enslow Publishers, Inc.

44 Fadem Road   PO Box 38
Box 699   Aldershot
Springfield, NJ 07081   Hants GU12 6BP
USA   UK
http://www.enslow.com

5958061

Library of Congress Cataloging–in–Publication Data

Torres, John Albert.
    Top 10 basketball three-point shooters / John Albert Torres.
       p. cm. — (Sports top 10)
    Includes bibliographical references (p. 46) and index.
    Summary: Examines the lives and careers of ten outstanding three-point
shooters in professional basketball history, including Michael Adams, Danny
Ainge, and Larry Bird.
    ISBN 0-7660-1071-6
    1. Basketball players—United States—Biography—Juvenile literature.
2. Basketball players—Rating of—United States—Juvenile literature.
3. Basketball—Offense—Juvenile literature. [1. Basketball players.] I. Title.
II. Title: Top ten basketball three-point shooters. III. Series.
GV884.A1T67 1999
796.323'092'2713
[B]—DC21
                                    98-3007
                                        CIP
                                        AC

Printed in the United States of America

10 9 8 7 6 5 4 3 2 1

Illustration Credits: Andy Hayt/NBA Photos, p. 21; Barry Gossage/NBA
Photos, p. 22; Chris Covatta, p. 30; Fernando Medina, p. 29; Glenn
James/NBA Photos, p. 45; Greg Shamus/NBA Photos, p. 25; Jerry
Wachter/NBA Photos, p. 19; Jim Cummins/NBA Photos, p. 17; Layne
Murdoch/NBA Photos, p. 42; Nathaniel S. Butler/NBA Photos, pp. 6, 10, 13,
15, 35, 37; Ray Amanti/NBA Photos, p. 33; Sam Forencich/NBA Photos, pp.
27, 39; Scott Cunningham/NBA Photos, pp. 9, 41.

Cover Illustration: AP/Wide World Photos

Cover Description: Reggie Miller of the Indiana Pacers

Interior Design: Richard Stalzer

CONTENTS

Introduction

THE THREE-POINT SHOT has become a potent weapon for most basketball teams. The number of good three-point shooters in the National Basketball Association (NBA) has forced teams to defend the outside shot. This means that the forwards and center are rarely double-teamed, and they have more chances to slam-dunk. All this translates into more excitement for NBA fans.

But what makes a great three-point shooter? Let's make a list.

First of all, a great three-point shooter has to have nerves of steel. He has to be willing to take a three-point shot with the game on the line.

Second, he must be quick and strong enough to be able to get open. The players call it getting a "good look" at the basket. The shooter's teammates must run plays that set screens and picks, allowing them to get open.

A great three-point shooter must also have good hands. He must be able to handle passes from every player on the team and through heavy traffic as well.

Most important, of course, the player must be a great jump shooter, because the three-point line is 29-feet 3-inches away from the basket. He must also be able to get the shot off quickly. Players today can catch a pass and shoot a three-pointer in a split second.

A three-point competition is now a regular part of the NBA All-Star weekend. The day before the All-Star game, some of the league's best shooters come together for this competition. The idea is to make the most three-pointers out of twenty-five shots, within the allotted time.

The shot was adopted by the NBA in 1980 as a novelty, but now it is a main part of most teams' offenses. Many coaches spend a lot of time coming up with offensive and defensive game plans based on the three-point shot and shooter. "It really puts pressure on a defense if a team can shoot the three, because it spreads the floor and it is more ground to cover,"[1] said NBA guard Terry Porter.

Statistics alone do not define this list of top ten three-point shooters. Instead, all ten players we have chosen, at one time or another, have been able to change how opposing teams prepare for them. They have been able to dominate games and put points on the board in a blink of an eye.

"The shot is a heartbreaker," longtime NBA coach Dick Motta said. "It has a psychological effect on the team and the opponent. If you make it, you can get fans involved in the game. If you're on the road, you can take them out of the game."[2]

CAREER STATISTICS

Player	NBA Seasons	Games	FG%	TPM	TPA	TPP	Pts	Average
MICHAEL ADAMS	11	653	.415	949	2,857	.332	9,621	14.7
DANNY AINGE	14	1,042	.469	1,002	2,651	.378	11,964	11.5
LARRY BIRD	13	897	.496	649	1,727	.376	21,791	24.3
DALE ELLIS	15	1,119	.481	1,588	3,949	.402	18,331	16.4
DAN MAJERLE	10	720	.440	1,046	2,875	.364	9,515	13.2
REGGIE MILLER	11	882	.485	1,596	3,950	.404	17,402	19.7
CHUCK PERSON	12	856	.461	1,141	3,118	.366	13,453	15.7
DRAZEN PETROVIC	4	290	.506	255	583	.437	4,461	15.4
MARK PRICE	12	722	.472	976	2,428	.402	10,989	15.2
DENNIS SCOTT	8	527	.419	1,106	2,774	.399	7,491	14.2

FG%=Field Goal Percentage
TPA=Three-point shots attempted
Pts=Points Scored

TPM=Three-point shots made
TPP=Three-point percentage
Average=Scoring average

*All statistics are through the 1997–98 season.

MICHAEL ADAMS

Michael Adams, then with the Washington Bullets, shows his fine shooting form.

MICHAEL ADAMS

NOVEMBER 19, 1992, WAS A SPECIAL NIGHT for Washington Bullets point guard Michael Adams. The Bullets were facing the Boston Celtics in Adams's hometown of Hartford, Connecticut. The five-foot ten-inch guard showed his great shooting form, scoring 40 points during a 126–118 victory. But it was what Adams did after the November 19 game of the 1992–93 season that proved he was truly a superstar.

Adams went out and bought two hundred turkeys. He then distributed them himself in his old neighborhood— just in time for Thanksgiving. "It was a nice thing," Adams said. "It really worked out. I like that."[1] It was not a surprise to those who know Michael Adams. He has always been known as a classy individual and a nice guy.

Michael Adams was born on January 19, 1963. His mother, Grace, worked long hours in the tobacco fields. His father, Oliver, was a factory worker on the night shift. Though his parents were very busy working, Adams received good teaching and guidance and was able to avoid the dangers of growing up in a tough neighborhood.

Adams played basketball at Hartford Public High School and soon became a star. He was the state's leading scorer as a senior, but incredibly, received no college offers. His lack of height scared away most of the big-name schools.

Adams was finally spotted at a summer all-star tournament in Bridgeport, Connecticut, by Kevin Mackey, an assistant coach at Boston College.

"I don't know what would have happened if I hadn't gotten that scholarship,"[2] he said. Adams led the BC offense for three seasons as the starting point guard. He showed many flashes of great shooting, and he was a good leader. He graduated in four years with a degree in speech communication, and his entire family drove to Boston to attend. He was the first person in his family to graduate college.

Because of his height, Adams was ignored until the third round of the 1985 draft. There, he was chosen by the Sacramento Kings. He made the team but rarely played, and in December the Kings let him go.

Adams played the rest of the season in the Continental Basketball Association (CBA). He played well and was signed by the NBA's Washington Bullets the following season. He was soon cut and then re-signed. He was traded to the Denver Nuggets in 1987. The Nuggets had big plans for Adams.

"We liked his speed," said Denver coach Doug Moe. "We wanted him, but he turned out to be so much more than we ever thought he could be."[3]

Adams became the NBA's all-time leader in three-point field goals made and attempted. He also ran off an incredible streak of 79 consecutive games with at least one three-pointer.

He led the league in three-point field goals for the 1988–89 season and the 1989–90 season. In 1990–91 Michael Adams was the league's sixth leading scorer, at 26.5 points per game. He also led the Nuggets in assists, steals, and minutes played. The Nuggets were a terrible team, however, and changes had to be made. Adams was traded closer to home when he rejoined the Bullets.

Adams played for the Charlotte Hornets in 1995–96, and that season proved to be his last. In a game dominated by much taller people, Michael Adams was constantly proving himself. Supposedly too little to play, Adams carved out an NBA career that most people only dream about.

BORN: January 19, 1963, Hartford, Connecticut.

HIGH SCHOOL: Hartford Public High School, Hartford, Connecticut.

COLLEGE: Boston College.

PRO: Sacramento Kings, 1985–1996; Washington Bullets, 1986–1987, 1991–1994; Denver Nuggets, 1987–1991; Charlotte Hornets, 1994–1996.

RECORDS: Shares single-game record for most three-pointers in one half, 7.

HONORS: Selected to All-Star game, 1992.

Driving to the basket, Adams looks to slip past the Atlanta defender. Adams finished his career with the Charlotte Hornets.

DANNY AINGE

Danny Ainge launches a three-point shot over the outstretched arm of Scottie Pippen.

ONLY FIVE SECONDS WERE LEFT in the game. Brigham Young University (BYU) was down by a point in the 1981 NCAA tournament against a tough Notre Dame team. BYU would try to get a good shot for their star outside shooter, Danny Ainge. Instead, Ainge took the inbound pass and made a mad dash. He dribbled the entire length of the court, through all five Notre Dame defenders, and laid the ball in for the winning basket. All in five seconds! It was a great play by a fiery competitor known to be good in the clutch, confident, and sometimes nasty.

In fact, Danny Ainge was always known as a bad guy, and he loved it. He was always the one player that opposing fans loved to hate. But he played basketball with a fire, a strong desire, and a great three-point shot.

"I got labeled as a villain and I started to love it," said Ainge, who is now the head coach of the Phoenix Suns. "It got me fired up on the road. And I'm not claiming innocence. I deserved some of it."[1]

Ainge was known throughout the NBA as a fiery spark plug. He was known as a player who constantly complained to the referees. He was also known as one of the most dangerous three-point shooters to ever play the game.

Daniel Rae Ainge was born on March 17, 1959, in Eugene, Oregon. He grew up loving sports. At North Eugene High School, he starred in basketball, baseball, and football.

Ainge was a basketball and baseball star at BYU. He was drafted by the Toronto Blue Jays to play baseball. Starting in 1979, Ainge played three seasons with Toronto but struggled with major-league pitching. His batting average for the three seasons was only .220, and he hit only 2 home runs. He continued to play college basketball at BYU after the baseball seasons were over.

The Boston Celtics drafted Ainge with the thirty-first pick of the 1981 draft. Ainge decided to quit baseball and give the NBA a try, but the Blue Jays did not want to let him out of his contract. The Celtics had to pay a lot of money to the Blue Jays to obtain Ainge's services.

When he got to Boston, Ainge joined a talented team that included Larry Bird, Kevin McHale, Nate Archibald, M. L. Carr, and Robert Parish. There were already a lot of star players on the team, so Ainge felt timid about taking shots.

"You're a bona fide shooter," Carr told him. "Pete Maravich and Jerry West got into the Hall of Fame by shooting the ball, and you've got to shoot the ball too."[2] Shoot the ball he did.

Ainge found that he was most comfortable behind the three-point arc. The Celtics had two of the league's best rebounders in McHale and Parish. They would be ready to grab the ball in case Ainge missed.

Danny Ainge was a main ingredient in two of Boston's championship teams. He led the NBA in 1987–88 when he made 148 three-pointers, for a .415 shooting percentage. His best scoring seasons were in 1988–89 and 1989–90, when he played for the lowly Sacramento Kings. He averaged better than 17 points a game for both seasons.

Ainge shot almost 38 percent from three-point range for his career, topping 40 percent four times. He made 150 treys in the 1992–93 season and made 40 percent of his attempts.

Danny Ainge retired after the 1994–95 season, after 6 trips to the NBA Finals and 2 championships. He did television work for a year before joining the Suns as a coach. Ainge coached with the same fire as he played. He led Phoenix to the playoffs during his first season as head coach.

DANNY AINGE

BORN: March 17, 1959, Eugene, Oregon.

HIGH SCHOOL: North Eugene High School, Eugene, Oregon.

COLLEGE: Brigham Young University.

PRO: Boston Celtics, 1981–1989; Sacramento Kings, 1989–1990;
Portland Trail Blazers, 1990–1992; Phoenix Suns, 1992–1995.

RECORDS: NBA playoff record for most three-pointers made, 172;
NBA playoff record for most three-pointers attempted, 433.

HONORS: Selected to All-Star game, 1988; Member of NBA
Championship team, 1984, 1986.

Ainge's three-point shooting helped guide the Suns to the 1993
NBA Finals. There the team played well but fell to the Bulls in
six games.

LARRY BIRD

WHEN LARRY BIRD LOOKED BACK at his basketball career, in August 1992, he shed a lot of tears. Bird had decided to retire from the game he loved so much.

There were so many memories that Bird could not sleep that night. They are the memories of one of the greatest basketball players ever to play the game. Yet Larry Bird almost didn't get a chance to play professional basketball.

Larry Bird was born on December 7, 1956, in West Baden, Indiana. Most children play basketball in the Hoosier state, and Bird was no exception. Bird became a star player at Springs Valley High School, in French Lick, Indiana. It was every boy's dream in French Lick, and throughout most of Indiana, to play basketball for Indiana University and its legendary coach, Bobby Knight. Bird was a last-minute recruit and did not commit until late spring.

Bird showed up at Indiana University and was immediately intimidated. He became homesick and hitchhiked back home twenty-four days later. He was broke, so he got a job driving a garbage truck and continued to play basketball in an amateur league.

Then, Bird's father, Joseph, committed suicide in 1975. It is something that haunts Bird even to this day. "I still can't believe it," he says. "All I can hope is that we'll meet up again someday."[1]

Indiana State University convinced Bird to give basketball another try. Larry Bird was an instant college superstar. He averaged 32.8 points a game and led his team to a 25–2 record. Bird was great again the next season, also averaging better than 30 points per game.

Before the defender can reach him, Larry Bird puts up a three-pointer.

In June 1978, Bird was drafted by the Boston Celtics, even though he still had another year of college ball left. This rule has since been changed. Bird played a final year at Indiana State. He led the Sycamores to the 1979 NCAA Championship Game. Bird scored 19 points, but Indiana State fell to Magic Johnson and the Michigan State Spartans. Then Bird finished his schooling, becoming the first person in his family to earn a college degree.

Larry Bird became an instant success in the NBA as well. He led his team to a 61-victory season during his rookie campaign. Bird was the choice as Rookie of the Year for the 1980 season.

Through the years, Bird led the Celtics to 3 world championships on the strength of his uncanny knack for the game and his long-range shooting. He was named the NBA's MVP three times, won 3 three-point shooting contests, and led the NBA in three-point field goals in 1985–86 and 1986–87.

Back problems late in his career forced Bird to retire in 1992. Bird's longtime rival, Magic Johnson, was the guest of honor the night that the Boston Celtics paid tribute to the retiring Bird. "I always told people that Larry Bird was the best all-around player that ever played the game," Johnson said. "But more than that, he was the one player I feared and respected more than anyone else."[2]

Bird spent a few years scouting and doing various tasks, but he had an interest in coaching. Bird took a job as head coach of the Indiana Pacers for the 1997–98 season.

Bird promptly did a great job coaching the Pacers. He led the team to the Eastern Conference Finals. The Pacers put up a good fight, but fell to the World Champion Chicago Bulls in seven games.

BORN: December 7, 1956, West Baden, Indiana.

HIGH SCHOOL: Springs Valley High School, French Lick, Indiana.

COLLEGE: Indiana University; Indiana State University.

PRO: Boston Celtics, 1979–1992.

RECORDS: NBA playoff record for most defensive rebounds, 1,323.

HONORS: NBA MVP, 1984–1986; NBA Rookie of the Year, 1980; All-
NBA first team, 1980–1988; Long Distance Shootout
winner, 1986–1988; NBA Finals MVP, 1984, 1986; Selected
to All-Star game, 1980–1988, 1990–1992; All-Star game
MVP, 1982; Member of NBA Championship team, 1981,
1984, 1986; Member of gold-medal-winning U.S. Olympic
team, 1992; Selected to NBA 50th Anniversary All-Time
Team.

Flying through the lane, Larry Bird floats a shot over Kareem
Abdul-Jabbar.

DALE ELLIS

DALE ELLIS CAME HARD AND FAST around a screen. He caught the pass, stopped dead in his tracks, and shot. The ball went right through the net as it had eight other times during the game. Ellis lifted his hands high over his head, indicating a three-point shot. It was his ninth try of the game.

At that time, Dale Ellis had made more three-pointers than anybody else in the history of the NBA. But never had he strung together so many three-pointers in a single game. It was April 20, 1990, and Ellis helped his Seattle SuperSonics teammates to a 121–99 victory over the Los Angeles Clippers. He scored 36 points in all and was 9 of 11 from behind the arc.

A night earlier, Ellis had lit up the Sacramento Kings with 43 points, including 7 three-pointers during a 130–118 rout for Seattle. It was an amazing two-game stretch, even for one of the game's deadliest shooters.

Ellis's secret formula for success is a rather simple one. "Practice, practice, practice," he said. "You can only improve by doing."[1]

During the off-season, Ellis takes roughly five hundred three-point shots a day. Once the season starts, he arrives at team practice before everyone else so he can take three hundred shots from behind the arc.

Dale Ellis was born on August 6, 1960, in Marietta, Georgia. He was always very athletic and played a lot of basketball. Ellis starred in high school and earned a scholarship to the University of Tennessee. There he established himself as a great college shooter.

DALE ELLIS

Skying for the ball, Dale Ellis grabs a rebound. Going into the 1997–98 NBA season, Dale Ellis was the all-time leader in three-pointers made.

The Dallas Mavericks made him the ninth player chosen overall in the 1983 draft. But Ellis did not make any big headlines for a while. At six feet seven inches, Ellis was expected to play small forward. But Ellis's game had always been better suited to play shooting guard. Since Dallas already had a great shooting guard in Rolando Blackman, Ellis soon found himself on the bench.

"We thought Ellis was the best senior in the draft that season," said Rick Sund, then the Mavericks director of player personnel. "He was the player to take at that spot."[2]

Things never worked out for Ellis in Dallas, and he asked to be traded. After three seasons, he was sent to the Seattle SuperSonics. That was where his career took off like lightning.

During the 1986–87 season, Dale Ellis scored 30 or more points in a game an astonishing 23 times. He also raised his scoring average by 17.8 points per game. He finished the season with the eighth-best scoring average at 24.9 points per game, up from 7.1 the previous year. He showed everybody that he belonged in the NBA.

Ellis's shooting and scoring average kept improving over the next few seasons. He averaged 25.8 points per game for the 1987–88 season for Seattle and then a whopping 27.5 points a game the next year. That season, Ellis also made 162 three-point baskets, shooting a lethal .478 percentage.

Over the years, Ellis has been traded a few times. He has played for Milwaukee, San Antonio, and Denver, in addition to Dallas and Seattle.

In 1996–97, Ellis averaged 16.9 points per game for the Denver Nuggets, including 192 treys and a .364 percentage. After the season, the SuperSonics made a trade with the Nuggets to bring Ellis back to Seattle.

Even after all his success, Ellis still sticks to his motto every single day: "Practice, practice, practice."[3]

DALE ELLIS

BORN: August 6, 1960, Marietta, Georgia.

HIGH SCHOOL: Marietta High School, Marietta, Georgia.

COLLEGE: University of Tennessee.

PRO: Dallas Mavericks, 1983–1986; Seattle SuperSonics,
1986–1991, 1997– ; Milwaukee Bucks, 1991–1992; San Antonio
Spurs, 1992–1994; Denver Nuggets, 1994–1997.

RECORDS: NBA single-game record for most minutes played.

HONORS: NBA Most Improved Player, 1987; Long Distance
Shootout winner, 1988; Selected to All-Star game, 1989.

More than just an outside threat, Dale Ellis was once one of the top
ten scorers in the league.

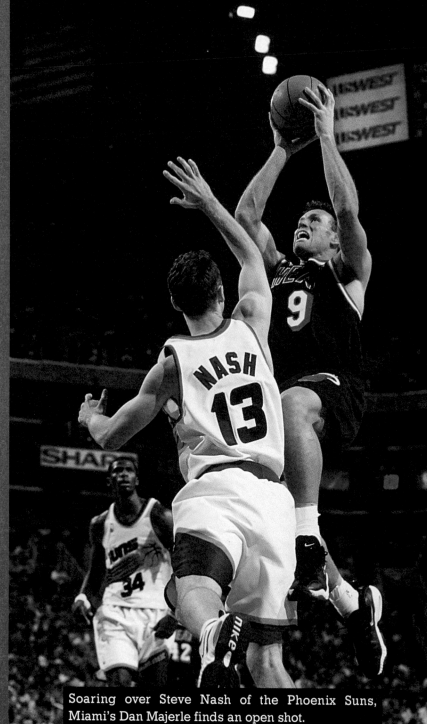

DAN MAJERLE

Soaring over Steve Nash of the Phoenix Suns, Miami's Dan Majerle finds an open shot.

THE GAME, THE SERIES, AND THE SEASON were all on the line. Phoenix Suns superstar guard Dan Majerle knew his team was in a shootout. The Seattle SuperSonics were leading the Western Conference Finals, three games to two. Majerle knew that it would take a great game to force a seventh game.

As usual, Dan Majerle came through. Majerle set an NBA playoff record by connecting on 8 three-point shots in ten attempts, to lead the Suns to a 120–114 victory. Majerle finished the game with 34 points. Majerle's magical shooting touch sparked his team to a victory in Game 7, as the Suns advanced to the championship series.

Dan Majerle was destined to become a great basketball player. He literally grew up with a basketball in his hands. His father, Frank, played basketball in a local recreational league. And when Majerle was just a baby, in Traverse City, Michigan, Frank would often toss a basketball into Dan's crib. Dan would grab the basketball and bite it.

Dan's mother, Sallie, didn't like her son playing with a dirty ball. "I'd holler, do you know how many germs are on that ball?" she said. "They must have been good germs, because Dan is very athletic."[1]

Dan Majerle was only five-feet, four-inches tall when he was a freshman at Traverse City High School. He had a natural shooting touch, so he became the team's guard. But he grew ten inches over the next two years, and he was moved to forward by his junior year.

Playing both positions was definitely a plus for Majerle.

He had to learn both positions and he had to work hard on all parts of his game—shooting, passing, and defense.

Majerle went on to play basketball at Central Michigan University. The school was not known for strong basketball teams, but he led his team to its first title in eight years. Majerle graduated in 1988 with a degree in physical education. The Suns had scouted him, and they liked the fact that he could play two different positions.

Not many of the Phoenix fans had heard of Dan Majerle when the team drafted him in the first round. Many of them booed. It did not take Majerle long to turn those boos into cheers. They began affectionately calling him "Thunder Dan" because of his crashing drives to the basket and his long three-point bombs.

The thing that makes Dan Majerle one of the greatest three-point shooters ever to play the game is that his opponent never knows what to expect. Many players will only shoot jump shots, but not Majerle. When he sees an opening, he will drive to the basket for a slam dunk. When he sees an open teammate, he will deliver a perfectly thrown pass. When he is left open by the three-point line, he will take the shot.

Dan Majerle led all basketball players in three-point field goals for the 1992–93 season and then again for the 1993–94 campaign.

Phoenix fans were disappointed when Majerle was traded to Cleveland in 1995. Majerle then signed with the Miami Heat prior to the 1996–97 season. Led by Coach Pat Riley, the Heat won the Atlantic Division. Majerle continued to provide his team with thunderous dunks and clutch three-point shooting.

"Dan is one of those guys," says former Phoenix coach Paul Westphal, "who just gives you whatever it is you need."[2]

DAN MAJERLE

BORN: September 9, 1965, Traverse City, Michigan.

HIGH SCHOOL: Traverse City Senior High School, Traverse City, Michigan.

COLLEGE: Central Michigan University.

PRO: Phoenix Suns, 1988–1995; Cleveland Cavaliers, 1995–1996; Miami Heat, 1996– .

RECORDS: Shares NBA Finals single-series record for most three-pointers, 17.

HONORS: Selected to All-Star game, 1992–1993, 1995; Member of bronze-medal-winning U.S. Olympic team, 1988.

Majerle puts the moves on the Pistons' Joe Dumars while Miami coach Pat Riley looks on.

REGGIE MILLER

THE FIRST GAME OF THE 1995 Eastern Conference Semifinals against the New York Knicks was just about lost. The Indiana Pacers found themselves down 105–99, with only eighteen seconds left in the game. Only a miracle could save them now—a miracle, or Reggie Miller. What happened next was truly amazing.

Miller cut the lead to 105–102 with a three-pointer from the left side with sixteen seconds still left to play. Then, Miller stole Anthony Mason's inbound pass, calmly dribbled back to the three-point line, and drilled another three-pointer, to tie the score at 105. Thirteen seconds remained.

The Knicks missed two foul shots and a jumper before fouling Miller, with seven seconds left. He made both foul shots, and the Pacers triumphed, 107–105. It was one of the most incredible come-from-behind victories in basketball history. The loss shook the Knicks, and they never recovered, losing the series to the Pacers.

Reginald Wayne Miller grew up on sports. He was born in 1965 in Riverside, California. He loved to play basketball and baseball, and he had two good role models. His older brother, Darrell, excelled at baseball and even made it to the major leagues. Miller's older sister, Cheryl, was one of the best women basketball players ever. She was a member of the gold medal-winning 1984 United States Olympic Women's Basketball Team and was inducted into the Basketball Hall of Fame.

"It was hard following Cheryl, but she helped motivate me tremendously," he said. "There was pressure, but it

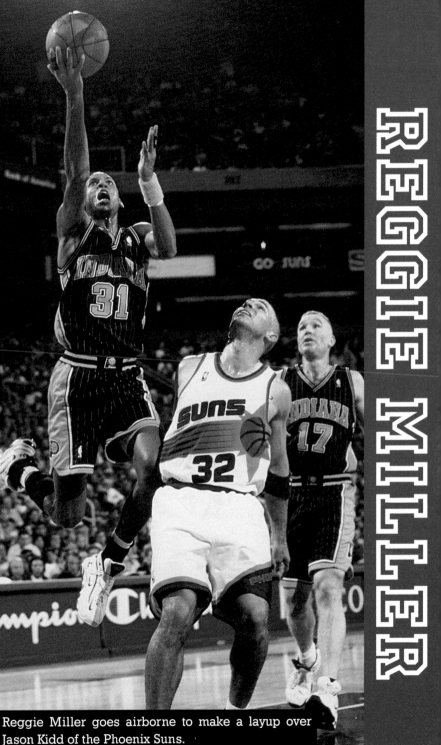

Reggie Miller goes airborne to make a layup over Jason Kidd of the Phoenix Suns.

helped me improve."[1] He credits Cheryl with helping him develop his great outside jump shot. She was the much taller of the two while growing up, and she would always block his shots. Therefore, Miller had to move farther away in order to be able to shoot. Then he started to grow taller when he went to Riverside Polytechnic High School.

Reggie Miller went to UCLA on a basketball scholarship. He improved every year and finished his four-year career with a 17.2 scoring average. But more importantly, Miller had gained the confidence that was needed to succeed in the NBA. "When I was at UCLA, [Lakers' players] Byron Scott, Magic Johnson, and Michael Cooper were the guys who took me under their wing and told me that I had what it took to make it in the NBA."[2]

The Indiana Pacers agreed. They made Miller their first-round draft pick, and the eleventh player chosen overall in the 1987 draft.

He averaged 10 points per game as a rookie and broke Larry Bird's record for three-pointers made by a rookie, tossing in 61. Two years later, Miller led the Pacers in scoring with a 24.6 scoring average and was selected to the All-Star team.

Now, the lanky, six-foot seven-inch, 195-pound guard is known as one of the best three-point shooters ever to play the game.

Reggie Miller's storybook career took another dramatic turn in 1996 when he was selected to the United States Olympic basketball team, also known as Dream Team III.

Miller helped his teammates capture the gold medal. He has also become Indiana's leading career scorer. His ultimate goal, however, is to bring a championship to the Pacers. While he tries, Miller will continue to nail three-point shots. During the 1997–98 season, Miller became the all-time leader in three-point field goals.

REGGIE MILLER

BORN: August 24, 1965, Riverside, California.

HIGH SCHOOL: Riverside Polytechnic, Riverside, California.

COLLEGE: UCLA.

PRO: Indiana Pacers, 1987– .

RECORDS: Holds NBA record for most three-pointers made; Shares NBA record for most seasons leading the league in three-pointers made; Holds playoff record for most three-pointers made in one quarter.

HONORS: All-NBA third team, 1995–1996; Selected to All-Star game, 1990, 1995–1996; Member of gold-medal-winning U.S. Olympic team, 1996.

Determined to get to the hoop, Reggie Miller brushes aside a Golden State defender. A prime-time player, Miller is known for his playoff heroics.

CHUCK PERSON

The Nuggets defenders can only wait for the result as Chuck Person shows them why he is nicknamed The Rifleman.

CHUCK PERSON

CHUCK PERSON, OF THE INDIANA PACERS, was going up against one of his rivals and good friends. Person and his Indiana teammates were facing Larry Bird and the Boston Celtics in the 1991 playoffs.

Chuck Person, known around the NBA as The Rifleman, guided the feisty Pacers to a tough five-game loss against one of the greatest teams ever. He led his team with 26 points per game. Bird and Person put on quite a show as two of the all-time greatest outside shooters squared off.

"From 15 to 16 feet out [away from the basket], Larry's better," Person said. "From outside the arc, there's no question who's better."[1]

Chuck Person has never been shy about his talent. In fact, over the years, he has earned a bad-boy image due to his finger-pointing, bragging, and trash talking.

"My high school coach told me that my on-court antics took away a lot of all-star type years,"[2] Person said.

One can't blame Person for enjoying himself and having fun. He has always had to live or play in someone else's shadow, and he has had to work very hard for everything.

Person was born on June 27, 1964, and grew up in Brantley, Alabama. His family was very poor. He learned about hard work at a young age. He took a part-time job to help his family by sweeping floors in the high school.

Person worked hard at basketball too. He became a high school star in Brantley, but he played in the shadow of Buck Johnson, who was considered the state's best player. Johnson later played for the Houston Rockets in the NBA.

Then after earning a scholarship to Auburn University,

Person was in the shadow of two other Auburn athletes: Charles Barkley and Bo Jackson. Person excelled in college. He made the South Eastern Conference (SEC) all-freshman team and was runner-up to Barkley for SEC Player of the Year. He made the United States Olympic team, as an alternate, and was runner-up for the scholar-athlete award.

"I've always been second best," Person said.[3] That's not entirely true. Person still holds many records at Auburn.

Person was booed when he was drafted by the Indiana Pacers with the fourth pick overall in the 1986 draft. The fans wanted Indiana to draft a big player, a center. Person said the booing was "hilarious." "I would have booed, too," he said. "But don't make a snap judgement until you see me play. If you like basketball, you'll love Chuck Person."[4]

Person showed what he was capable of right away. He averaged 18.8 points per game, led the team in minutes played and in three-pointers, and was second in rebounds with 8.3 and second in assists with 3.6.

For the first time, Person was not second best. In 1987, he was voted the NBA's Rookie of the Year.

Person became known as one of the NBA's best catch-and-shoot players. Strangely, he is not a great foul shooter. He piles up his points from the outside.

Person spent many years with Indiana, before playing for the Minnesota Timberwolves and most recently the San Antonio Spurs. As a part-time player for the Spurs, Person made 190 three-pointers in 1995–96 for a .410 percentage.

Chuck Person provides his team with instant offense when he comes off the bench.

Even though he is no longer considered a star, Person is still confident in his ability. "Not only will I take the shot," he said, "I'll make it. I feel I can make every shot."[5]

CHUCK PERSON

BORN: June 27, 1964, Brantley, Alabama.

HIGH SCHOOL: Brantley High School, Brantley, Alabama.

COLLEGE: Auburn University, Auburn, Alabama.

PRO: Indiana Pacers, 1986–1992; Minnesota Timberwolves,
1992–1994; San Antonio Spurs, 1994– .

HONORS: NBA Rookie of the Year, 1987.

Keeping his eye on the action, Chuck Person is set to play defense. Person knows that it takes more than three-point shooting to become a successful NBA player.

DRAZEN PETROVIC

CONSISTENCY AND RESPECT were the two things that Drazen Petrovic always strived for. One time, during his rookie season Petrovic was floored by an elbow thrown by Blue Edwards of the Utah Jazz.

The bony-framed Petrovic jumped to his feet and confronted the bigger Edwards. "You play correct or we will fight!" he shouted.[1]

Drazen Petrovic was always tough. In many ways, he had to be. He was born on October 22, 1964, in Croatia, in the former Yugoslavia.

When civil war broke out in Croatia, Petrovic's only escape was basketball. Smaller than many of the other players, Petrovic often had to defend himself and prove to others that he belonged.

By the time he was twenty, Drazen Petrovic was one of the best players in the Yugoslav League. In one game, he scored an incredible 112 points.

Petrovic was drafted in the third round by the Trail Blazers in 1986 but continued to play in Europe for the next few years. He was a member of the Yugoslavian silver-medal-winning Olympic basketball team in 1988.

When Petrovic reported to the Trail Blazers in 1989, he had a hard time adjusting to the very physical play of the NBA. Petrovic had a tough time working his way through picks and holding his own on defense. He averaged a respectable 7.6 points a game as a rookie, but after two years he was not playing much. Petrovic finally asked Portland to trade him to a place where he could get more playing time.

His body square to the basket, Drazen Petrovic displays his perfect three-point shooting form.

DRAZEN PETROVIC

Around midseason, on January 23, 1991, Portland traded Petrovic to the New Jersey Nets. He was determined to make the most of his new opportunity and to earn the respect of his new teammates. Petrovic spent the off-season working out constantly.

Petrovic became an instant crowd favorite in New Jersey. He became the team's best scorer, averaging 20.6 points per game, and he proved to be one of the league's best three-point shooters.

In the summer of 1991, Petrovic joined fellow country-man and NBA player Toni Kukoc at the Barcelona Summer Olympics. Petrovic's play led Croatia to a silver medal, finishing just behind America's Dream Team.

The next season, chants of "Petro, Petro" thundered at the New Jersey Nets home games. He finished the season as the NBA's eleventh leading scorer, with a 22.3 average, and he was third in the league in three-point shooting, with a .449 percentage.

When the 1992–93 season ended, Petrovic was still determined to show everyone what a great player he was. He would work on his game even more. Then tragedy struck; Petrovic was killed in an automobile accident on a rainy highway in Germany. He was twenty-eight years old.

Drazen Petrovic made 255 three-point field goals in his very brief NBA career. His shooting percentage from three-point range was one of the best ever at .437.

Nets' general manager and Hall of Famer Willis Reed cried when he heard the news about Petrovic. "To me, it's like losing a son," he said. "I saw a lion-hearted player. Petro came from a small country, but he worked to play basketball at the level of Americans."[2]

DRAZEN PETROVIC

BORN: October 22, 1964, Sibenik, Yugoslavia.

DIED: June 7, 1993, Germany.

COLLEGE: University of Zagreb, Zagreb, Yugoslavia.

PRO: Portland Trail Blazers, 1989–1991; New Jersey Nets,
1991–1993.

HONORS: All NBA third team, 1993; Member of silver-medal-winning
Yugoslavian Olympic team, 1988; Member of silver-
medal-winning Croatian Olympic team, 1992.

Struggling to get the shot off, Drazen Petrovic leans into his
defender to make some room. Sadly, Petrovic died in an auto
accident, thus cutting short a potentially great career.

MARK PRICE

ALL-STAR POINT GUARD MARK PRICE is used to the pressure of big crowds. His teammates have always counted on him in important situations. But nothing prepared him for the pressure and excitement he felt in front of seventy thousand people in June 1994.

Price had been asked by his idol, the Reverend Billy Graham, to speak at a religious rally at Cleveland Stadium. He was very nervous, but he agreed to do it. "I never had a hero," he said. "At least not a basketball hero. There were players I liked, but no one I wanted to emulate. The man I most admired and always wanted to meet was Billy Graham. Even when I was a kid I felt like that."[1]

Mark Price was born on February 15, 1964, in Bartlesville, Oklahoma. He grew up with a basketball in one hand and a Bible in the other. He had good training in both. His father was an assistant basketball coach at the University of Oklahoma and then with the Phoenix Suns. His family was also very involved in the church.

Like many of today's great NBA shooters, the six-foot Price had to overcome his lack of size to make it. He credits hard work and religion.

Price starred in high school, but his game took a dramatic turn for the better when he rededicated his life to God. "During my junior year in high school," he said, "I began to realize that the goals I'd set for myself weren't fulfilling me like I thought they would. So I began seriously looking at my belief system."[2]

He went from being a star to being a superstar and earned a basketball scholarship to Georgia Tech, which

MARK PRICE

Sprinting down the court, Mark Price leads the Warriors' fast break.

plays in the very competitive Atlantic Coast Conference. Price became the first freshman ever to lead the ACC in scoring, with a 20.3 average. Price averaged better than 15 points a game for all four of his college seasons, and he scored 17.4 points per game as a senior. He was also an accomplished point guard who was comfortable in dishing the ball out to his teammates and making the offense click.

Because of his height, Price was not chosen until the twenty-fifth pick of the second round, by the Dallas Mavericks. His draft rights were traded to the Cleveland Cavaliers almost immediately.

Price has always been more concerned with making his teammates better with good passes than with his own statistics. "I've always believed that if you do well as a team then the individual rewards are going to come," he said.[3]

The rewards came during Price's second season with the Cavs. He was named the starting point guard, and he had a great season. He averaged 16.0 points per game and piled up 480 assists. As Price gained more confidence in his ability, his shooting improved. Soon he was regarded as one of the game's most dangerous three-point shooters.

Price has played in four All-Star games and is one of the all-time leaders in three-point field goal percentage. Price was also named to the United States National basketball team, otherwise known as Dream Team II, in 1994. He helped them win the World Championship of Basketball. The team won 8 games by an average margin of victory of almost 40 points. "That," said Price, "was a great experience, not only to represent my country, but to play with the incredible talent assembled on that team."[4]

The quiet Christian, Mark Price, continues to let his shooting do his talking as he enters into the latter part of his spectacular NBA career.

MARK PRICE

BORN: February 15, 1964, Bartlesville, Oklahoma.

HIGH SCHOOL: Enid High School, Enid, Oklahoma.

COLLEGE: Georgia Institute of Technology, Atlanta, Georgia.

PRO: Cleveland Cavaliers, 1986–1995; Washington Bullets, 1995–1996; Golden State Warriors, 1996–1997; Orlando Magic, 1997– .

RECORDS: NBA career record for highest free-throw percentage; NBA career playoff record for highest free-throw percentage.

HONORS: All NBA first team, 1993; Long Distance Shootout winner, 1993–1994; Selected to NBA All-Star game, 1989, 1992–1994.

Mark Price goes in for an easy two. Price has battled back from serious injuries to continue his NBA career.

DENNIS SCOTT

Dennis Scott has always been known for his long range shooting ability. His nickname is 3-D, because of his three-point shot.

DENNIS SCOTT

DENNIS SCOTT HAD ESTABLISHED HIMSELF as one of the great three-point shooters of his time. But there was a time when his Orlando Magic teammates were looking for his shooting touch more than ever.

The 1995 Eastern Conference Finals against Reggie Miller and the Indiana Pacers was quickly turning into a three-point shootout. After winning the important first game of the best-of-seven series, the Magic seemed on the verge of losing Game 2 and with it their home court advantage. That's when Scott, known as 3-D to his teammates and friends because he's such a great three-point shooter, took over. He made a clutch 7 of 15 three-pointers, to lead the Magic to a 119–114 win.

Scott had been in a minor shooting slump before the game and joked afterward that he had taken some shooting advice from center Shaquille O'Neal. The truth of the matter is that Scott worked hard to get out of his slump. He stayed up late before Game 2, shooting his jump shot on a court near his house, under the glow of a single streetlight.

Preparation is nothing new for Scott. He practices his three-point technique by taking very short shots. He slowly backs up until he feels comfortable at a particular spot. Eventually, he winds up behind the three-point line. Scott finishes practice by taking three hundred three-point shots.

Dennis Scott likes to offer advice of his own to young basketball players. "Step forward while you're shooting and always follow through," Scott said. "Sometimes you'll know before the ball leaves your hands if you're going to make it. To become a good three-point shooter you have to have confidence in yourself. If I get a good look at the basket, I feel that I should hit the shot every time."[1]

Dennis Scott was born on September 5, 1968, in Hagerstown, Maryland. He became a star player for Flint Hill Prep Academy in Oakton, Virginia. As a high school senior, Scott was named the Naismith National Player of the Year. He was good enough to earn a scholarship to Georgia Tech.

Scott left Georgia Tech after three years. He was the fourth player drafted in the first round of the 1990 draft by the Orlando Magic.

Dennis Scott had a very good rookie season, averaging 15.7 points a game. He showed his excellent shooting touch with a .425 shooting percentage and a .374 percentage from the three-point range.

Scott likes to get the crowd excited by hitting a three-pointer. "My three's are like one of Shaq's monster dunks," he said. "It really gets the crowd into the game."[2]

On April 18, 1996, Scott really got the crowd into the game when he connected on 11 three-pointers to break the NBA single-game record. He knocked down 11 of 17 shots, leading Orlando to a 119–104 victory over the Atlanta Hawks. Scott, who finished the game with 35 points, left the game to a rousing standing ovation.

That same season Scott shattered the single-season record by hitting 267 three-point field goals. His shooting percentage from behind the arc was an amazing .425.

"You can't leave Dennis Scott open," claims former teammate Nick Anderson. "He can shoot it—and hit it—from the locker room."[3]

DENNIS SCOTT

BORN: September 5, 1968, Hagerstown, Maryland.

HIGH SCHOOL: Flint Hill Preparatory Academy, Oakton, Virginia.

COLLEGE: Georgia Institute of Technology, Atlanta, Georgia.

PRO: Orlando Magic, 1990–1997; Dallas Mavericks, 1997–1998; Phoenix Suns, 1998– .

RECORDS: NBA single-season record for most three-pointers made; Shares single-game record for most three-pointers made.

HONORS: NBA All-Rookie first team, 1991.

Dennis Scott puts the ball on the floor in a game against the Utah Jazz.

Chapter Notes

Introduction
1. David Moore, "Hot Shots: In the NBA, the 3-Point Shot is Trey Bien," *The Sporting News*, December 11, 1995, p. 41.
2. Ibid., p. 43.

Michael Adams
1. Leigh Montville, "Mighty Mike," *Sports Illustrated*, January 20, 1992, p. 53.
2. Ibid., p. 52.
3. Ibid., p. 53.

Danny Ainge
1. Tom Feikin, "No More Knocking the Suns," *The New York Times*, December 20, 1996, p. B18.
2. Ibid.

Larry Bird
1. Peter May, *The Big Three* (New York: Simon & Schuster, 1994), p. 27.
2. Ibid., pp. 278–279.

Dale Ellis
1. Walter Roessing, "Shooting Stars," *Boys Life*, January, 1995, p. 16.
2. Jack McCallum, "The Joy of Getting Even," *Sports Illustrated*, May 4, 1987, p. 30.
3. Roessing, p. 16.

Dan Majerle
1. "Dan Majerle: Guard/Forward Phoenix Suns," *Sports Illustrated for Kids*, April 1994, p. 45.
2. Phil Taylor, "Rolling Thunder," *Sports Illustrated*, June 14, 1993, p. 39.

Reggie Miller
1. Curtis Bunn, "Miller Scores 8 Points in Last 16 Seconds as Pacers Rally to Beat Knicks," Knight-Ridder/Tribune News Service, May 7, 1995.
2. *NBA Hoops Collect-A-Books*, JBC, 1990.

Chuck Person
1. Tim Kurkjian, "Chuck Person," *Sports Illustrated*, November 7, 1994, p. 148.

2. Ibid.

3. Douglas S. Looney, "A Very Special Person," *Sports Illustrated*, January 12, 1987, p. 89.

4. Ibid., p. 88.

5. Kurkjian, p. 148.

Drazen Petrovic

1. Scoreboard Obituary, "Drazen's Legacy," *Sports Illustrated*, June 21, 1993, p. 13.

2. Obituary, "Died: Drazen Petrovic," *Time*, June 21, 1993, p. 19.

Mark Price

1. Terry Pluto, "Basketball Star Mark Price is Proud of his Religious Faith and Values," Knight-Ridder/Tribune News Service, June 17, 1994.

2. "Cool Under Pressure," *Campus Life*, May/June 1995, p. 39.

3. *NBA Hoops Collect-A-Books*, JBC, 1990.

4. "Cool Under Pressure," p. 39.

Dennis Scott

1. Ben Kaplan, "Great Scott!," *Sports Illustrated for Kids*, June 1996, p. 26.

2. Sam Goldaper, "Nets Make Coleman No. 1 Pick in NBA Draft," *The New York Times*, May 25, 1990, B20.

3. Ibid.

INDEX